Set Aside to be a Bride

Mrs.Coretha McCall

A King's Daughter Publishing Company LLC.

Set aside to be a Bride

Copyright©2014 A King's Daughter Publishing Company LLC

Published by A King's Daughter Publishing Company LLC

Peachtree City, Georgia

Scripture quotations are from the King James Version.

ISBN: 978-1483969893

Printed in the United States of America

Dedication

To My Aunt Johnetta because of your obedience unto God my life has been changed forever.

Thank You for inviting me that day I will never forget it.

I Love You!

Continue in the good fight of faith.

I Timothy 6:12

Special Thanks

To the women of God that helped me get this done I could
not have done this without you!

Lisa Randolph, Christina Bush, Salena Epps-Jackson

To my Loves, my Family

Thank You to my man of God, my Husband Durrell for your
love and support and my two beautiful little girls for loving
their Mommy.

Acknowledgements

To my Pastors

Dr. Creflo Dollar and Taffi Dollar you have truly made my life easier as a Christian. Thank you for teaching the word of God with simplicity and understanding. You taught it in a way where I could apply it to my life and live it out victoriously!

Contents

Preface

In using the analogy of a Bride preparing for her wedding day, I hope this book will give you guidance to help you meet the perfect bridegroom; so you can enter into the Kingdom of heaven and not be shut out! So if you're ready you can start sending out the invitations now because this will be the wedding of the city, state and the world! Your guest will be glad to receive this invitation. They will want to know this very special bridegroom because He is perfect!

Introduction

The reason I wrote this book was to let people know how much God loves and cares for them. He made a way for us to be connected to Him and live forever. He gave the ultimate sacrifice through sending his son Jesus to die on the cross for our sins to ensure once and for all that we could have access to Him daily. We can now rest assure that this relationship will last forever but it will all depend on you. You see He knows what He wants, but the question is do you know what you want? When God created us He put a longing desire in each of us to be committed to Him, however when we allow other things to take His place we get stuck. We get stuck in unfulfilled relationships and connections with things thus, we begin to lose hope. God is Faithful. He has always been faithful to us and He will never leave us. If we accept his love (Jesus) we will be married to the most faithful God we will ever know and be in the most loving and beautiful relationship ever. You don't have to worry about Him even if you have been hurt before you can trust him.

Chapter 1

The Purpose of the Marriage

God's purpose for marriage is to join two people together in a committed covenant relationship as Husband and wife, companions, partners, and friends for the rest of their lives until death. As a married couple there are a lot of great things you can do together. You can enjoy each other's company, live together, have children, build businesses and ministries to help others, take care of each other, and start a legacy together for your children and grandchildren. Now I'm not saying that everybody feels this way or even marries for this reason but if you ask the average person what they are seeking in a marriage they are looking for commitment.

Likewise, when you get involved in a personal relationship with Jesus it should be better. Yes this is a relationship and not religion because He can love you back, protect you, encourage you, and you can really trust him because he always keeps his word no matter what. The purpose of this marriage would be a great experience for you because you will get unconditional love and have everlasting life no matter how you look, how much you weigh, or whether you have a job or not just to name a few.

John 3:16

For God so loved the world, that he gave his only begotten Son, that whosoever believeth in him should not perish but have everlasting life.

You see when you come to know him you will benefit in so many ways and gaining eternal life is only the beginning.

The Proposal

Will you marry me? These are the four words of the one who has decided in their mind that they want to spend the rest of their life with you and only you. This person believes in their heart that you are the one who will stick with them for better or worse, for richer or poorer, in sickness and health, until death do you part. Because of what they believe in their heart, they make a confession with their mouth and pop the big question. Likewise, to become a bride you must Confess with your mouth and believe in your heart that God has raised Jesus from the dead.

Romans 10:9, 10

9 That if thou shalt confess with thy mouth the Lord Jesus, and shalt believe in thine heart that God hath raised him from the dead, thou shalt be saved.

Is this the right time?

When you first meet someone traditionally you would ask a lot of questions, meet the family and you would likely take some time (weeks, months or even years?) to decide if this is the person you want to spend the rest of your life with. Well when you meet this special person it would definitely be an exception! There is no time to think about whether you want to be with Him or not. The time is now! This is the time to get in this committed relationship because later may not be an option.

Romans 13:11

And that, knowing the time, that now it is high time to awake out of sleep: for now is our salvation nearer than when we believed.

Matthew 25:13

Watch therefore, for ye know neither the day nor the hour wherein the Son of man cometh.

Great things are waiting in your future. There is so much that begins to take place once the decision is made. I'm telling you I am a witness to it; my life has drastically changed ever since I met Him. To be honest with you this is the best life to live. Now don't get me wrong I do have my challenges sometimes however I still have peace and joy.

If you have never received Jesus as your Lord and Savior repeat this prayer

Jesus I Believe you are the Son of God. I believe God raised you from the Dead come into my heart I receive you now in Jesus name Amen.

Welcome into the God's family!

Daily Confession:

Thank you Lord I am a child of God and you love me just the way I am right where I'm at.

Chapter 2

The Bride and Bridegroom

Traditionally in a wedding ceremony the Beautiful Bride is the focus of the wedding, it is all about her. While the the details of the wedding are important like the cake, decorations, and so on nothing is more important than the Bride because without her there is no wedding! Isn't she lovely! Isn't she wonderful! The bride is priceless. She is priceless because of what was paid for her by the blood of Jesus, the price that was paid can never be repaid it cost that much!   God set out to never be separated from us the whole world could be a Bride if they chose to.

The Bride
After you have received Jesus you are now the Bride. Congratulations! You are the one he is coming back for so get ready!

John 3: 16, 17

For God so loved the world that he gave His only begotten Son, that whosoever believeth on him should not perish but have everlasting life.

17 For God sent not His Son into the world to condemn the world; but that the world through Him might be saved.

Romans: 10:13

For whosoever shall call upon the name of the Lord shall be saved.

The Bridegroom

When the Bridegroom is ready to marry he wants to do what it takes to make her happy. This perfect Bridegroom is an exception he not only wants to see his Bride happy but has an unconditional, undying, and unfailing love. He thought it out, He counted the cost, and He is always ready and willing to love His Bride.

John 3:29

He that hath the bride is the bridegroom: but the friend of the bridegroom, which standeth and heareth him, rejoiceth greatly because of the bridegrooms voice.

John 14: 3

And if I go and prepare a place for you, I will come again, and receive you unto myself; that where I am ye may be also.

How much will this wedding cost?

Normally you would set a budget for your big wedding day but in this case you pay Absolutely Nothing, it's Free! I hear people say all the time there is nothing in life for free, well they are all wrong because this gift is FREE. Take a look for yourself.

Ephesians 2:8

For by grace are ye saved through faith; and that not of yourselves: it is the gift of God.

There is nothing that you can repay or give to cover this gift. You cannot **work** for it or earn it! It is freely given. He loves you that much!

Chapter 3

The Perfect Dress!

(Renewing your mind)

Your wedding day is important and you want to make sure everything is exactly how you want it. So you begin to look for the perfect dress, you may look at 5 to 10 dresses before you decide on the perfect one. During this process you may get the opinions of several different people who are close to you in your life such as your mother, sister(s) or your Best friend. All of these questions and more will arise as time goes on including how much it cost! Well just like you go through that process to make the right decision for your dress, there is a process you will go through also in your mind. Putting on a new way of thinking is exactly what needs to happen when you become a Born-again Christian. This new way of thinking can only be attained by the word of God. Your renewed mind will be your perfect dress!

Romans 12:2

And be not conformed to this world but be ye transformed by the renewing of your mind, that ye may prove what is that good, and acceptable, and perfect will of God.

An old way of thinking equals an old way of living. When you become a Christian you should not continue to be the same old person you were before you received Jesus Christ. Your new thinking is what sets the stage for a new way of living.

Testimony 1

Before receiving Jesus into my life I observed people around me saying they were Christians but acted just like me. I was not interested in God or his Son one bit. Besides, at the time I really did not see any reason to give my life to this Jesus they were talking about. I didn't see any difference between them and myself. However, after giving my life to Him I learned over time that you had to do more than attend church for your life to change. I learned that we must read the word of God daily and apply it to our lives for this to happen. It is important as a Christian to live a life that represents God; we don't want to discredit who He is by acting the opposite way of what the word of God says about us. This transformation of your mind will not happen all at once. The Bible is our instruction manual for our new way of life.

Testimony 2

I can remember when I first started studying my Bible it was so empowering after reading the words for myself it became personal and intimate. My faith began to grow and a strong desire to change my perspective about men began to happen. One of my greatest struggles in the beginning of Christianity was getting over the hurt and pain of the absence of a father. I desperately wanted to have him in my life. Because I Struggled with rejection it always caused me to be in some kind of relationship even when I didn't really want to be. Oftentimes, I still felt unfulfilled and unhappy going through the motions with an emptiness in my heart. As I began to read the word of God, He began to bring understanding about the emptiness I was dealing with. Over time the emptiness began to fill with the Love of God. My broken and hardened heart began to drink the life from the pages of His word. As I continued to read my thinking was changed by the beautiful words.

2 Corinthians 5: 17

Therefore if any man be in Christ, he is a new creature: old things are passed away: behold all things are become new.

If you decide not renew your mind by ready your Bible **you will become relig**ious and burned out of going to church in no time. What do I mean by religious? I mean you will be acting as if you are connected to God because of your weekly church attendance but that will be it, everything else will be the same this type of life can leave you feeling hopeless and frustrated.

2 Timothy 3:5

Having the form of Godliness but denying the power thereof: from such turn away.

You study for an exam in school, if you don't pass that exam you will have to repeat the class. The purpose for studying for the exam is to get promoted. This will lead you to graduation to begin to fulfill your purpose. Likewise, the reason for you renewing your mind with the word of God is to produce that good, acceptable, and perfect will of God that will promote you to greater things in your life and cause others to want this new life also.

The most important thing is to get the word in your heart! Listen to it, sing it, and speak it. While it may seem small to you it's a change for the better which means you are growing. So continue my Brothers and sisters to read! Now if you're saying I don't even know where to start, this is a big book! I would say just start and don't break off more than you can chew. You can start out with a couple of verses at a time. Whatever you choose to do study it to get an understanding.

Testimony 3
Thinking back there were few people available to take me by the hand and explain to me what I you needed to do. I remember feeling lost and asking myself, where is the

support system for this new life? In the first few years as a new Christian I struggle understanding the process. At church I heard many sermons about how much God wanted to bless me but nobody told me you had to get the word inside your heart to receive those things.

James: 1:22-25
But be ye doers of the word, and not hearers only, deceiving your own selves. For if any be a hearer of the word, and not a doer, he is like unto a man beholding his natural face in a glass: for he beholding himself, and goeth his way, and straightway forgetteth what manner of man he was. But whoso looketh into the perfect law of Liberty, and continueth therein, he being not a forgetful hearer, but a doer of the work, this man shall be blessed in his deed.

It's a continual process to get to the special day, be confident, do it with all your heart, mind, soul and strength. People will not recognize you because you will begin to think, talk, and act different. Your process may vary depending what you have been through. No two people processes are the same however, the word of God will always be the same. You will be so thankful at the end if you don't abort the challenge and deal directly with whatever is in your heart. Issues of the heart can stop the process. So my encouraging words to you are follow through with the challenge you can do it!

Life Application: Please no condemnation!

If you get into sin at any time in your relationship please do not hang around with condemnation repent quickly. It should not be in your circle at all! If you are hanging around with others who may be trying to condemn you pray quickly for them because they don't realize that condemning others opens themselves up to being condemned.

Romans 8: 1

There is therefore now no condemnation to them which are in Christ Jesus, who walk not after the flesh, but after the Spirit.

James 5: 9

Grudge not one against another; brethren, lest ye be condemned; behold, the judge standeth before the door.

You now belong to God and Jesus is your Savior so you never have to accept condemnation. We belong God who forgives as soon as we repent. So don't waddle around in whatever you did wrong and don't allow others to hold you down in the sin by reminding you every time of your past mistake. People are people. Don't be put into bondage. When you mess up and know it repent quickly because your Father in heaven loves you and He is merciful.

Ephesians 2:4

But God who is rich in mercy, for his great love wherewith he loved us;

I understand now more than ever that God's love is real. He is the same all the time. He is always ready to embrace and love on you but you have to be willing to receive. God is ready to love no matter how many times you mess up. GOD LOVES YOU!

Testimony 4
There were times when I knew I did or said something wrong. However, I repented quickly so that the enemy would not have access to my mind and caused me to feel condemn or be able to hinder my life. I would keep it moving after that and God restored me.

1. Do you know and believe God and His Son love you

no matter what?

2.   If not why?

Are you struggling with a particular sin?

Would you like to be free from condemnation repeat this:

Prayer

I repent for the sin I committed and turn away from it I ask for forgiveness. Lord I say right now I am free from condemnation I choose not to walk in this. I am free from every sin, guilt, and shame associated with the past sin. Thank you for your forgiveness Amen.

Chapter 4

The Best Man and the Gift

(Holy Spirit and the gift)

When the Bridegroom gets married traditionally he has a best man which is usually someone that is a close friend, He is the chief attendant at the wedding. The best man represents a bond of trust between the two. He is there for comfort and support, the best man knows this groom better than anybody. He is there to make sure the Bridegroom has everything just the way it is supposed to be. Likewise, Jesus has someone similar to a best man named the Holy Spirit. Holy Spirit is part of the wedding to make sure that the Bride knows what the Bridegroom wants. Holy Spirit will lead and guide you into all truth and bring things to your remembrance to assist you so that you are sure to be in God's will.

John 14:26

But the Comforter which is the Holy Ghost whom the Father will send in my name he shall teach you all things and bring all things to your remembrance whatsoever I have said unto you.

John 16:13
Howbeit when he, the spirit of truth is come he will guide you into all truth: for He shall not speak of Himself but whatsoever He shall hear, that shall he speak; and he will shew you things to come.

He shows you what to do when you don't know what to do, He helps you to pray when you don't exactly know what you want to say and the list can go on! How do I know all this, it's in the Book! Having the Holy Spirit in your life is like having extra protection with you. You need the Holy Spirit because you cannot afford to miss out on anything and just like those five foolish virgins who slept and slumbered waiting around I believe that this is what they were missing! Let's take a look again at the scripture:

Matthew 25: 2

2 Now five of them were wise, and five were foolish. 3 Those who were foolish took their lamps and took no oil with them, 4 but the wise took oil in their vessels with their lamps. 5 But while the bridegroom was delayed, they all slumbered and slept.6 "And at midnight a cry was heard: 'Behold, the bridegroom is coming; go out to meet him!' 7 Then all those virgins arose and trimmed their lamps. 8 And the foolish said to the wise, 'Give us some of your oil, for our lamps are going out.' 9 But the wise answered, saying, 'No, lest there should not be enough for us and you; but go rather to those who sell, and buy for yourselves.' 10 And while they went to buy, the bridegroom came, and those who were ready went in with him to the wedding; and the door was shut.11 "Afterward the other virgins came also, saying, 'Lord, Lord, open to us!' 12 But he answered and said, 'Assuredly, I say to you, I do not know you.'13 "Watch therefore, for you know neither the day nor the hour in which the Son of Man is coming.

As you could see they were called foolish because they did not have extra oil. The extra oil that the wise virgins carried with them was a representation of the Holy Spirit. The foolish virgins based there decision off of only what they knew. They did not have all of the insight about what was going to occur. Foolish people lack wisdom and understanding. They do what they want, when they want. They don't ask questions because they think they are right. Foolish people do not listen to Godly counsel.

Proverbs 18:2

A fool hath no delight in understanding, but that his heart may discover itself.

This is exactly how they got shut out of the wedding. Although they were right there with the wise they had the nerve to lay around and sleep! Now that foolish!

Matthew 25:5
5 But while the bridegroom was delayed, they all slumbered and slept.

Even if you don't know what to do acknowledge Holy Spirit and ask for help and you will know what to do. I have prayed before and said "O.K. Holy Spirit I don't know what to do about this situation in..." And after a while (it may take minutes, hours, or days,) I received the wisdom that I needed to make good decision.

Life Application: "No cliques for Brides"

The foolish virgins remind me somewhat of clique they hang together only to pull each other down. When choosing friends as you continue to progress in your walk with Jesus seek out people who are bearing "good fruit" in character and conversation. Stay clear of people who murmur and complain about the pastor, and other people in the church or who just act plain old foolish. Most of the time these cliques are formed by people who are hurt or walking in some kind of offence and they attract others who have similar characteristics as them. Hurt people need to be healed by Jesus and until that happens they can divide the local church and cause major confusion full of gossip and lies while spreading the hurt all around. Use wisdom and pay attention! This group becomes a type of clique. Cliques operate out of offense they have been hurt and gravitate towards others who have issues similar to them. Don't get entangled with this type of group. Once you hear the talk of gossiping, backbiting, jealousy, envy, and hatred just to name a few you better run. If you are trying to be accepted and don't disconnect from them it is only a matter of time before you are acting like the group.

I Corinthians 15:33

Be not deceived: evil communications corrupt good manners.

This is not a group you want to be accountable to. This can be a time when offense can slip do to the negative behavior of others   but do not allow this to happen if you come across a situation like this makeup in your heart to forgive quickly and pray for them. Doing this keeps you free. Freedom has been given to you by Jesus However, you have to make an effort to keep it.

The Evidence of Speaking in tongues

I remember a conversation with another Christian about how to pray, she shared how sometimes she does not know what to say when she is praying. So I ask her, "Do you know about the Holy Spirit? She said, "No." I said, "would you like to meet the Holy Spirit and receive the Gift of the Holy Spirit with the evidence of speaking in tongues?" and she said," no… I'm not ready for that right now." I showed her in the scriptures where it was from Jesus in the books of Acts. After showing her all the signs and wonders that followed after the Holy Spirit came she still said no. My opinion is that this response comes from two things, fear of not knowing what you're saying and the "odd" behavior people observe during the time of prayer. This "odd" behavior gets stereotyped by onlookers in negative ways. People make fun and connect it with the activity of the devil. They did the same thing in the book of Acts they said they were drunk.

If you read the first chapter of the book of Acts as you read you will see that Jesus told his disciple to wait for the Holy Spirit (the promise from God the Father).

Acts 1:5, 8

5 For John truly baptized with water; but ye shall be baptized with the Holy Ghost not many days hence.
8 But ye shall receive power after that the Holy Ghost is come upon you and ye shall be witnesses unto me both in Jerusalem, and in all Judea, and in Samaria, and unto the uttermost part of the earth.

Jude 20
But ye beloved, building up yourselves on your most Holy faith, praying in the Holy Ghost, Keep yourselves in the Love of God looking for the mercy of our Lord Jesus Christ into eternal life.

Did you see that! When you're praying in the Holy Ghost although you may not know what you are saying it is strengthening you on the inside, building your faith up to stand strong in adversity, and giving you confidence in your faith in Jesus Christ.
Because I was a new Christian and having challenges Mrs. Maria was my prayer buddy.
This was a culture shock to my thinking, it was not going the way I wanted to and Maria would encourage me to pray more about the situation. Not knowing exactly what to pray I began praying in the Holy Ghost and over time I saw things begin to change.

Praying in the Holy Ghost will also keep you in the love of God. There will be times when you will come into contact with people that you will not like or even want to love!

Praying in the Holy Ghost will give you the power to break those negative emotions that comes from others as well as yourself. The Love of God is necessary in order to have relationships. This is how people know who you belong too. Love is your signature that you are a child of God.

Praying in the Holy Ghost gives you Power to win others to Jesus Christ. In the Book of Acts you can see the power of the Holy Ghost in which Peter and many other Disciples were able to win thousands to the Body of Christ.
After that the Holy Spirit fell upon them and they spoke in other tongues this was the evidence that showed the power of God. So if you have a desire to have this power ask the Holy Spirit to become active in your life with the evidence of speaking in tongues and begin to thank the Lord for the activation of it and pray. You may be wondering or asking how do I know if I'm praying in the spirit? Why does it sound like this? Just keep praying. If you are a born again Christian and you acknowledge the Holy Spirit and ask for the evidence of speaking in tongues it will eventually come. Do not stop praying or give up if you did not experience this immediately it takes time for some people.

When I first received the Gift of the Holy Spirit with the evidence of speaking in tongues I was at church. My pastor asked if anybody in the congregation wanted to receive this gift. I went to the front and he laid his hands on my shoulders and said repeat after me, after I finished repeating the prayer I began to thank God. Suddenly words I never heard before began to flow from my lips. It was one of the most awesome experiences to hear myself speak a language I had never heard before until that moment. The power of God is contagious.

Questions to consider

1. Would you like to receive the gift of the Holy Ghost with the evidence of speaking in tongues?

2. If not why?

3. Do you acknowledge the Holy Spirit?

4. If not why?

Chapter 5
The Wedding Party

(Discipleship and accountability)

I remember going through this part of getting prepared for my wedding choosing those you love to be a part of this BIG day is never easy because there are so many family members and friends that you are connected to and you don't want to leave anybody out. However, you know that you cannot pick everyone. So how would you choose who's the bridesmaids or groomsmen? Would it have to do with whether they are your siblings, cousins, or best friends? Would it all be based on who you have the best relationships with or would you weed them out based on who you don't like, maybe have disagreed with in the past or maybe recently?

Well however you go about it, it's one of those things that has be done unless you choose to get married without a wedding party period. In my own opinion your wedding party should be made up of people who have affected your life positively and caused you to grow and mature. Now you may not agree and that's quite alright. It's just my opinion and this is what leads me to discuss the importance of Discipleship and Accountability when you are a born again Christian.

I believe all Christians need to be connected to someone they can be accountable to about their growth or lack of growth as a Christian. You may be thinking Discipleship and Accountability? That process went away with Jesus a long time ago! A Disciple is a follower of Jesus Christ, we are still doing it today. These days I see Christians who turn away and go back into the world and one of the reasons I believe is due to a lack of accountability and discipleship, this helps the person become successful and effective in life as a Christian.

These days there is a rush to see quick results and if it's not fast enough we keep moving on to something or someone else. Unfortunately, this is a part of life. For this reason we have all of these people who give their life to Jesus everyday but they don't have other Disciples in place to help guide them along the way. God thinks we are worth every bit of the time it takes.

Likewise, in preparation for the ultimate wedding you have to decide who you will be accountable too. Usually these people would need to be those that you liked, loved, and trusted. This particular group of people would be allowed to speak into life and give you good sound Godly counsel. The wedding party is supposed to represent a group of people who will support, pray and have the best interest for you marriage relationship.

For instance, if you have a problem in your marriage they would say, "Let's pray". The people would genuinely have your back! Likewise, there should be someone you can go to in confidence to help and support you when you need it. Because in this relationship with Christ it will not always be easy for you as your relationship develops. I would like to refer to these friends as your Accountability. Everyone in the Body of Christ regardless of what Denomination needs someone they can go to for prayer or whatever is needed to help them to grow and progress in their relationship with God. These are the people that can get in your business! If you wrong, they can correct you. If you're going the wrong way they can lead you back on course. Let me tell you, YOU NEED THESE KIND OF PEOPLE!

Proverbs 19:20

Hear counsel and receive instruction that thou mayest be wise in the latter end.

In this day and time the Enemy (Satan) is attempting to do his best to get Christians alone and distracted with all kinds of tricks. This is where doubt and confusion can slip in and take us in a totally different direction away from the will of God. In this doubtful and confusing state we can begin to speak and operate as if Jesus will not return and reap consequences that we will regret in the end. I believe this is what the foolish did not have accountability and it took them further and further away from God until they were known as foolish. I believe they received warnings along the way but refused to listen. As they continued to walk in this state of mind they found others like them to validate their thinking and behavior

QUESTIONS TO CONSIDER

1. Do you have a friend or Friends you are accountable to?

   Do they help you stay on track?

2. Do they speak words of hope?

3. Do you feel like they have your best interest?

4. Do you feel comfortable sharing your personal information with them?

If you desire to have some accountability you can trust in your life to assist in making you better as a Christian repeat this:

Prayer

Lord I thank you for your great love. I ask that you send some Godly accountability partners to help me continue my growth with prayer and Godly Counsel Amen.

Chapter 6

Communication is everything

(Prayer)

In marriage you will need to get to know the other person because there will be things that you will need to know and the only way to do is to communicate. If you did not talk to your spouse and only lived with them it would be hard for you to have a lasting marriage. Communication is a very intimate thing and it is underutilized in marriage relationships today. I have heard so many people say they don't really communicate with their spouse after they get married well... not like they use to anyway. I have heard people say it becomes "business as usual" after the honeymoon stage. Yeah you know what I mean "got to pay the bills" and that's what the focus of the relationship becomes all about. Keep those lights on, pay that house note, pay that car note because love alone can't do all that right?

Communication or what I would like to call Prayer is vital in your relationship with Jesus. Your prayer time is what draws you closer to Him because it is so intimate. You are holding these personal conversations telling Him all about you dreams, hopes, and desires and he is taking it all in quietly listening to every single word. All His attention is on you and he shares it with his Father THE ALMIGHTY GOD.

Now keep in mind when you're praying it's not all about talking but it is also about listening too. Prayer is a tool you do not want to be without ever. It is in prayer that you get wisdom, understanding, clarity, and answers to your problems. Listening for the voice of the Good Shepherd can lead and guide you in the right direction.

John 10:14

I am the Good Shepherd, and know my sheep, and am known of mine.

Proverbs 3:5, 6

Trust in the Lord with all thine heart; and lean not unto thine own understanding. In all thy ways acknowledge him, and he shall direct thy paths.

Make up in your mind and heart that prayer will be a great part of your everyday life. Personally, I pray all through the day I just speak out to Jesus just like he is standing in front of me. I share all of my hurts, pains, concerns and anything else I can think off. It is that easy. In my experience I have heard many different variations of ways that I should pray and what I have found that works for me was just being transparent about what is in my heart. No hidden agendas, motives or secrets just being honest about what is in my heart and believing in faith that he hears me. It has done me a world of good to be able to trust God enough to release all of that stuff to Him. God did not create us to carry those things you know. He wants us to be free. Free to worship, free to live day to day in Him without any hindrances or cares weighing us down.

Questions to Consider

1. **Do you pray daily?**

2. **Do you have a desire to pray?**

3. **Do you pray only when things are going wrong?**

   If you have a desire to communicate with God more repeat this:

   Prayer

   Lord help me I desire to come closer through prayer to you to get to know you better Amen.

Chapter 7

The Pastor

Traditionally in preparing for a wedding you would have to decide who would officiate the wedding. Some people decide to go to the court house some people may get married in their backyard whatever you decide they would need to be someone who was qualified to marry you and the bridegroom. In order for your marriage to be recognized as a legal union the person needs to have some qualifications such as license which is acknowledged by the state you live in. This license proves to the state that they are qualified to legally marry two people in Holy Matrimony. This person has the authority by the state to pronounce you husband and wife, they sign your marriage license and you are now Mr. and Mrs. Such and such.

Likewise, when preparing for the big wedding day to the perfect bridegroom Jesus it is important that you have someone sent by God to preach and teach the word of God to you. A pastor helps assist in building your faith by rightly dividing the word of God so that you can understand it and apply it to your life. A pastor also watches over your soul through prayer and assist in guiding you in the right direction. The Bible tells us that faith comes by hearing and hearing by the word of God that comes through a Preacher let's take a look at the scripture.

Romans 10:14-15,17

How then shall they call on him in whom they have not believed? And how shall they believe in him whom they have not heard? And how shall they hear without a preacher? 15 And how shall they preach except they be sent? As it is written, how beautiful are the feet of them that preach the gospel of peace and bring glad tidings of good things! 17 so then faith cometh by hearing, and hearing by the word of God.

As you can see a Pastor is supposed to be sent by God to assist in bringing people to Jesus Christ. It is through the preaching of the word that people call on the name of the Lord and become saved. The Preacher gives Hope to those that hear the word of God. The people get hope in what is being preached which builds faith and expectation in what they heard. So if you are not attending a local church then I would like to encourage you to pray and seek the Lord and as your are seeking start to visit places where you can hear the gospel of peace with glad tidings of good things! It is a great place not only to hear the word but also great opportunities to build relationships and make friends.

Questions to consider

1. Do you attend a local church?

2. Do you understand the word that is being preached? If not why?

If you want to attend a local church were you can grow as a Christian and build your faith repeat this:

Prayer

Lord I ask you to begin to show me where I need to attend church. As I go out to visit different places show me your perfect will for me Amen.

Chapter 8

The Big Wedding Day

Well it's the big day! You have stayed focused and you have let your light shine, shine, shine throughout this process! The Bridegroom is ready for his Bride, and all who were called to be there will attend. There were so many different options you could have chosen for this day such as: Hawaii, a beautiful beach, a church, a courthouse, or maybe even your backyard. The choices were endless. However, this wedding is extremely different there is a beautiful place already prepared for the awesome day. It is called Heaven. That's right this place is not like anything you have ever seen before and I mean that literally. Instead of the music playing "Here comes the Bride" you will actually hear the sound of trumpets letting you know the Bridegroom is here! Jesus tell us that he goes to prepare a place for us to come. It's all set up with priceless decorations such as gold and pearls and every other jewel you could imagine!

John 14:2, 3

In my Father's house are many mansions: if it were not so I would have told you. I go to prepare a place for you.3 and if I go and prepare a place for you, I will come again, and receive you unto myself; that where I am, there ye may be also.

Revelation 21:21

The twelve gates were twelve pearls: each individual gate was of one pearl. And the street of the city as pure gold, like transparent glass.

This is what you have been preparing for all this time!

A word of encouragement from the Author

While this book is not exhaustive in its information of all the various ways that you can live a victorious life. I pray that it will help you know matter where you are in your life. Pray for those around you that you see are struggling whether it's in their conversation, lifestyle etc… Make sure that you are and will represent the best that you can!

Galatians 6:1, 9

Brethren, if a man be overtaken in a fault, ye which are spiritual, restore such a one in the spirit of meekness; considering thyself, lest thou also be tempted.

As we have therefore opportunity, let us do well unto all men, especially unto them who are of the household of faith.

This book is for those who may be feeling like what's the use in all this. I can remember going through this exact process the monotony and routine of it all. Well this feeling can come from several reasons such as 1. Not digging deeper into the word 2. Wanting what others have or what others are doing 3.trying to stay connected to the world and its way of doing things or 4. Not seeking God on what you should be doing and then actually doing it! This is all a part of the process of Growing into a mature Christian and it takes patience and time. Stand through the process don't give up because you will see the end result if you don't quit or cave in.

Daily Confession to live a Godly lifestyle.

Father God thank you for your Son Jesus. Thank you for giving me everlasting life through him. I declare in Jesus name that I am your child and I know your voice. I am submitted to your will and follow through in obedience and faith. I can do all things through Jesus Christ who strengthens me even though it may seem hard. I am blessed because I seek Godly counsel therefore, I make good decisions for my life. I surround myself with people who love and seek after God and His Son Jesus. I am not a hearer only acting religious, deceiving myself, but I am a doer of the word of God. I acknowledge God in all my ways and apply the word of God to every area of my life on a daily basis. I declare I am wise like the five virgins full of wisdom and understanding. I love God with all my heart, mind, soul, strength and I purpose to represent God and His Son well by loving my neighbor as I love myself. I will demonstrate the love of God and will not condemn others for their mistakes. I will not speak corrupt words only encouraging words that will lift the person who hears and minister grace to them. I am a God lover and a people lover I am victorious!

Scriptures:

Philippians 4:13

Psalms 1:1

James 1:22

Proverbs 3:5, 6,

Ephesians 4:29

Matthew 22:37

Set aside to be a Bride